4

The WINNERS

ONE FOR ALL ALL FOR ONE Teachers UNITED

10

SCHOOL TEAM

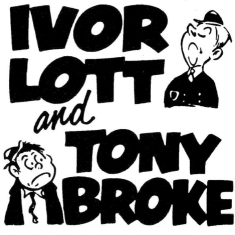

IVOR LOTT and TONY BROKE

HULLO, IVOR! WHAT DO YOU WANT WITH A RUNNING TRACK?

HUH! I'M A SUPERB ATHLETE! ...I'LL CHALLENGE YOU TO A FEW CONTESTS...IT'LL BE GOOD PRACTICE FOR THE SCHOOL SPORTS!

OKAY!

AND SO...

BANG

FIRST, THE HURDLES! WE'RE OFF!

STOP TALKING AND RUN!

I'M WINNING!

NOT FOR LONG!

THEN...

SNIGGER!

HEY! MY HURDLES ARE GROWING! AND IVOR'S ARE GETTING LOWER!

TRIP

OOF!

THE WINNER! HO, HO!

CRASH

THEN...

I'LL BEAT YOU AT THE POLE VAULT, IVOR!

WE'LL SEE!

HERE GOES!

THAT POLE LOOKS A BIT SMALL, IVOR!

HOW'S THAT?

STRETCH

HUH! A STRETCHING POLE! CHEATING AGAIN!

NEXT...

GROAN! THIS SHOT IS HEAVY!

HEFT

I WIN AGAIN!

HUH! THAT SHOT OF IVOR'S MUST BE POUNDS LIGHTER THAN MINE!

30 CENTIMETRES, YOU ARE A WEAKLING, RIFF-RAFF!

BONK

ROLLLLL

THE WINNER MUST GET HIS MEDALS... SOLID GOLD OF COURSE!

HUH!

1 VOR

2

3

LOWEST SCORE

RAISE MY FLAG, RIFF-RAFF!

EH?

3

LOWEST SCORE

HURRY UP!

H'M! SO THAT'S WHERE MY SHOT LANDED!

YANK

SPIN

L

CRUMP!

CRACK

OOPS!

CRASH!

IVOR! GRR!

RUN, IVOR! RUN!

AAAGH! I CAN'T!... THESE GOLD MEDALS ARE WEIGHING ME DOWN!

17

CLEVER DICK
THE DAFT INVENTOR (AND NAPOLEON DOG)

FLIPPING JIMMY GREEN'S FISHING FOR GOLDFISH FOR HIS CAT IN OUR POND!

CLEAR OFF AN' LEAVE OUR FISH ALONE!

SNIP

I'LL BE BACK! I WANT SOME FISH FOR MY CAT!

AND I'LL BE READY FOR YOU!

LATER...

NO SIGN OF DICK... HELLO, WHAT A FUNNY FISH!

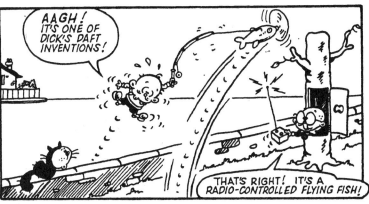

AAGH! IT'S ONE OF DICK'S DAFT INVENTIONS!

THAT'S RIGHT! IT'S A RADIO-CONTROLLED FLYING FISH!

EVEN LATER...

I THINK DICK'S GONE OUT!

GUIDED MISSILE

BONK

OH, NO I HAVEN'T! LIKE MY SUBMARINE?

I'LL CHASE HIM OFF ONCE AN' FOR ALL IF HE COMES BACK!

EVEN LATER STILL...

DICK MUST THINK I'M DAFT! THE LOCH NESS MONSTER COULDN'T FIT IN HIS POND!

BEWARE OF THE LOCH NESS MONSTER

BEWARE OF THE LOCH NESS MONSTER

AAGH! IT IS THE LOCH NESS MONSTER!

HELP! MUM!

HE WON'T BE BACK!

MARTIN BAXENDALE

20

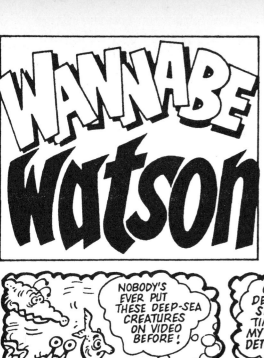

Tom Thug's Skooldayz

28

Helpful HETTIE

32

33

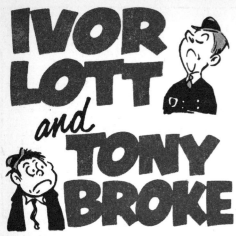

DRACULA DOBBS

42

The Scruffs...

TOP of the CLASS

Melvyn's Mirror

BEASTENDERS

ANGIE AND KATH ARE DOING SOME SHOPPING IN THE WEST END...

WE'RE WEARING THESE MASKS OVER OUR FACES SO WE WON'T SCARE THE HUMANS!

THEN... TRY THIS NEW LIPSTICK, MADAM!

OKEY-DOKEY!

BUT...

OOPS! I'VE SMASHED THE MIRROR!

CRASH! TINKLE!

LET'S GET OUT OF HERE BEFORE SOMEONE RECOGNISES US!

SWAMP MONSTERS — THE MOST FRIGHTENING HORROR FILM EVER MADE!

THAT SOUNDS GOOD, ANGIE!

WE MAY EVEN HAVE RELATIVES IN IT!

BUT...

HAW, HAW! THIS FILM'S REALLY PATHETIC!

HEH, HEH! BEST LAUGH I'VE HAD FOR AGES!

YOU'RE RUINING THE FILM!

BAH! HOW DARE YOU THROW US OUT!

RIGHT, KATH! LET'S SHOW 'EM SOMETHING REALLY FRIGHTENING!

YES! I'M GETTING SICK OF HIDING BEHIND MASKS ALL THE TIME!

SO...

AAAGGHH!

HELP!

THEN...

THE BEASTENDERS ARE HERE!

DRIVE THEM OUT!

SWAMP MONSTERS — THE MOST FRIGHTENING HORROR FILM EVER MADE!

This way, kids →

49

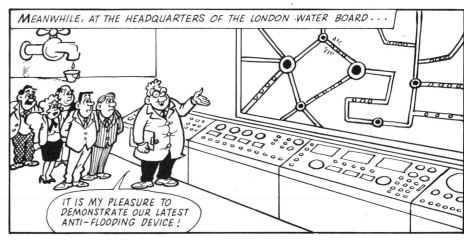

50

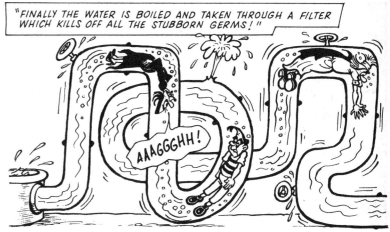

CLEVER DICK
THE DAFT INVENTOR (AND NAPOLEON DOG)

Martin Baxendale

WALT TEASER

58

KID KONG

HOLIDAY RELIEF

WORKER REQUIRED for General Duties in BANANA WAREHOUSE APPLY WITHIN

THAT FOR KID! EARN LOTS OF MONEY!

I'LL SEE YOU WHEN YOU GET HOME— FULL OF BANANAS, NO DOUBT!

SO...

KID HERE! LEAD ME TO THE 'NANAS!

HO-HO! NOT SO FAST, KID! I'LL SHOW YOU YOUR FIRST TASK!

YOU'VE TO UNLOAD AND STACK ALL OUR NEW BANANA BOXES! THEY'LL BE FULL OF BANANAS ONE DAY SOON!

OOO! OKAY! SOONER KID GET STARTED, SOONER KID GET FINISHED!

AND SOON...

OKAY! NOW KID GET TO 'NANAS?

NOT YET, I'M AFRAID! FOLLOW ME!

THESE BILLS HAVE TO GO OUT AND THE ENVELOPES HAVE TO BE LICKED!

GLEEP! WHETHER KID LICK IT OR NOT! CHUCKLE! JOKE!

GASP! THAT YUKKY-TASTING WORK! NEED 'NANAS TO TAKE GUM AWAY!

'FRAID NOT! YOU HAVE TO WASH OUR BANANA LORRIES FIRST!

ACHE!

THEY'RE ALL IN TONIGHT, AND WE LIKE TO KEEP THEM SPOTLESSLY CLEAN!

YOWP! THAT MORE LORRIES THAN KID EVER SEEN!

THAT NIGHT...

HELLO, KID! IT IS 'NANAS FOR TEA...

...OR ARE YOU SO FULL OF THEM YOU COULDN'T FACE ANY MORE?

KID WORKED IN 'NANA WAREHOUSE ALL DAY AND NOT EVEN SEEN A PESKY 'NANA! KID STARVING!

HUH?

62

63

The PARK

PARKY, I'D LIKE TO DISCUSS SOME **WORK** WITH YOU!

SWOON!

STAGGER!

WE NEED A LIST OF EVERY TREE IN THE PARK, SAYING **WHERE** IT IS AND WHAT **KIND** IT IS!

GIBBER! TWITTER!

TWITCH!

TRUST THE PARKS CHAIRMAN TO USE A VERY UNFORTUNATE WORD IN FRONT OF PARKY...

SO, ONE REVIVING GLASS OF WATER LATER...

TREES? I'VE NEVER EVEN **LOOKED** AT THEM BEFORE! I DON'T KNOW ONE FROM ANOTHER! I **HATE** TREES!

DISGUSTED MUTTER!

PSST! THIS COULD BE FUN!

THE GROT STREET GANG LEARNT ABOUT TREES AT SCHOOL! WE'LL HELP!

COO! TA!

THAT IS OBVIOUSLY A **LEMON** TREE!

SCRIBBLE!

PSST! THEY ARE OLD **PLASTIC** LEMONS THAT YOU GET JUICE IN FROM SHOPS!

PAH! I'D HAVE KNOWN THE LEMON TREE, OF COURSE! WHAT'S NEXT?

I'LL SHOW YOU!

SNOOTY SNIFF!

GOSH, I DIDN'T KNOW THAT THERE WAS A **SHOE TREE** HERE! WHEN THEY'RE PROPERLY RIPE, THEY'LL BE **CLOGS!**

GOODNESS ME! MIND YOU, I'VE **HEARD** OF A SHOE TREE, OF COURSE!

YOU KNOW HOW YOU GET ALL DIFFERENT KINDS OF JAM... EVER HEARD OF A **LOG JAM?**

LOG JAM... YES, I HAVE!

WELL, THAT'S THE TREE THAT IT COMES FROM!

GASP! I NEVER KNEW WE HAD ONE OF THOSE!

GIGGLE!

LOOK! GRANDPA SQUIRREL AT THE TOP, PARENTS BELOW, AND CHILDREN ON THE BRANCHES UNDER THAT!

SO WHAT KIND OF TREE IS THAT?

—TOM PATERSON—

64

GUESS WHO ISN'T VERY POP'LAR WITH PARKY—BUT THEY'RE NOT GOING TO PINE OVER IT!

Just JOKING

WHY IS THAT WINDOW CRYING?

BECAUSE IT HAS A PANE!

WHAT IS A BEE'S FAVOURITE COMIC?

BUZZTER!

WHAT'S YELLOW AND WRITES?

A PENANA!

FLEA CIRCUS

GINGER

The small cat with the BIG appetite!

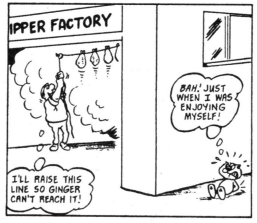

FACEACHE
AT BELMONTE SCHOOL

RIGHT, YOU LOT! FOR ONCE, YOU'RE GOING TO CONTRIBUTE SOMETHING TOWARDS THE GOOD OF HUMANITY INSTEAD OF DRIVING IT SCATTY! YOU'RE ALL GOING TO BECOME *BLOOD DONORS* LIKE ME!

WHAT!

YOU CAN COUNT *ME* OUT! I FAINT AT THE SIGHT OF A BOTTLE OF TOMATO SAUCE! (GULP!) THE FACT THAT I'VE GOT A BODY *FULL* OF BLOOD MAKES ME CRINGE!

THEN YOU CAN *CRINGE* WHILE YOU'RE *DONATING* BECAUSE THE BLOOD BANK VAN'S CALLING AFTER LESSONS AND YOU'LL ALL ASSEMBLE IN THE SCHOOL YARD AT 5 O'CLOCK SHARP WITH YOUR SLEEVES ROLLED UP!

!

AFTER LESSONS...

WHAT'LL WE DO? I DON'T WANT TO BE A BLOOD DONOR— WHAT BIT I'VE GOT I'D RATHER HANG ON TO!

ME, TOO! I DON'T MIND SHARING ANYTHING WITH ANYBODY—'CEPT ME BLOOD!

CALM DOWN, FELLERS— I'VE JUST HAD A GREAT IDEA!

HEH-HEH! ALL I NEED NOW IS A SCHOOLMASTER'S BLACK GOWN— PLUS A SCRUNGE!

SHORTLY...

I'VE BORROWED A GOWN! NOW TO CREEP UP TO SNIPE'S ROOM WHILE HE'S HAVING HIS AFTERNOON NAP!

KNOCK KNOCK

SCRUNGE

COME IN!

BLISS

THANK YOU, SIR! SORRY TO DISTURB YOU BUT I'VE COME TO COLLECT YOUR BLOOD!

EH..? WHAT..?

!

IT'S A NEW NATIONAL HEALTH SCHEME TO SAVE PETROL! THEY'RE SENDING *US* ROUND INSTEAD OF THE VAN!

AGHH! GAD! A VAMPIRE!

GIBBER-GIBBER

COME BACK! IT WON'T HURT! JUST A QUICK NIP ON THE NECK!

HORROR

ZOOM

HOSPITAL? STRIKE US OFF YOUR LIST OF BLOOD DONORS! *HUMANITY CAN LUMP IT!*

AND AT 5.30, IN THE SCHOOL YARD...

IT'S OKAY, FELLERS! YOU CAN ALL ROLL YOUR SLEEVES DOWN! THE VAN WON'T BE COMING!

Helpful HETTIE

80

IT'S A Nice Life

ALL WAS PEACEFUL ON THE NICE FAMILY'S PLOT— UNTIL...

WHACK!

THUMP!

WHOA! STOP!

CALM DOWN, ANIMALS!

WHERE DID THIS GOLF-BALL COME FROM?

SORRY! I WAS JUST GETTING IN SOME PRACTICE BEFORE MY ROUND OF GOLF THIS AFTERNOON!

WHOA! COME BACK, DUSTBIN! MR. JONES CAN'T HELP BEING A ROTTEN GOLFER!

ROTTEN, EH? AT LEAST I CAN PLAY THE GAME, WHICH IS MORE THAN YOU CAN DO!

WELL... IF I HAD SOME GOLF-CLUBS...

HMM... I KNOW— I'LL MAKE MY OWN, THAT'LL SHOW HIM!

THAT'S THE WAY, DAD!

CHIP! CHIP!

AND...

WHO NEEDS THOSE FANCY CLUBS? I CAN PLAY JUST AS WELL WITH THIS ONE!

GOLF CLUB PRACTICE AREA

BUT...

OOPS!

1ST TEE

ZUNK!

DONG!

OW! HIM AGAIN!

AAARGH!

BLAM!

WHACK!

I SAY! WHAT A SHOT!

PLOP!

SO...

YOU'RE RIGHT, OLLIE, YOU ARE BETTER AT GOLF! I'D HAVE NEVER MANAGED A 'HOLE IN ONE'!

NICE TRADITION OF BUYING EVERY-ONE ON THE COURSE A MEAL TO CELEBRATE, TOO!

PITY YOU CAN'T SIT DOWN AND JOIN US! CHUCKLE!

FUME!

CLUB HOUSE

THROB!

BILL FOR CELEBRATION MEAL

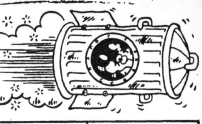

CLEVER DICK
THE DAFT INVENTOR (AND NAPOLEON DOG)

85

94

IVOR LOTT and TONY BROKE
with MILLY O'NAIRE and PENNY LESS

SID BURGON

97

TEST YOURSELF

ARE YOU IMPULSIVE?

To find out, answer each of the questions, tick the appropriate one, then check your score, pals!

1 Morning, and in the playground the school bully is picking on a little kid from your class. Do you. . .
A. Dash over to side with your classmate?
B. Go and look for a teacher to take charge?
C. Keep well out of it?

2 A dishy classmate gives you a nice birthday present. Do you. . .
A. Thank him/her politely, but don't draw attention to it 'cos of the sarky comments you'll get from the others?
B. Play it so cool that you appear to be ungrateful?
C. Give him/her a big, smacking kiss on the cheek?

3 Teach asks who would like the afternoon off lessons. Do you. . .
A. Say nothing 'cos there's bound to be a catch, like picking up all the litter in the school?
B. Immediately thrust your hand in the air, yelling "Me! Me!"?
C. Ask Teach if there are any 'strings' attached?

4 4 o'clock, and on the way to buy a Wham! album you see a man selling fantastic-looking watches from a suitcase. Do you. . .
A. Blow your money on a watch that he tells you acts as a calculator, alarm, stop-watch and also plays Wham! hits?
B. Ask to examine a watch, and find out if it's got a guarantee?
C. Say nothing is going to stop you from buying the record?

TURN THE PAGE TO CHECK YOUR SCORE

14–20
You always act on the spur of the moment, and this often results in clashes. On the other hand, there's never a dull moment!

6–13
You're quite excitable, but you've found that it can get you into trouble. You try to restrain yourself, but don't always succeed!

0–5
You are the cautious type, who carefully examines the pros and cons before doing anything. Try to loosen up a little!

1. A–5, B–3, C–0; 2. A–2, B–0, C–5; 3. A–0, B–5, C–3; 4. A–5, B–2, C–0.

LEW STRINGER